Ballycastle
County Antrim 1954

GW00775614

**Ballycastle 1954, County Antrim**

**A Clachan Reproduction**
Republished by Clachan Publishing
3 Drumavoley Park, Ballycastle, BT54 6PE, County Antrim.

IBSN: 978-1-291-32497-6

Email                info@academic-collections.com
Website:   http://clachanpublishing-com.webs.com/

**Clachan Publishing** is a printing service dedicated to the preservation and promotion of print material related to Irish local and family histories. We publish memoires, articles, collections of old photographs, old letters, papers, newspaper cuttings, brochures, scrapbooks, - anything at all - that may be of local or family interest.

We rely largely on materials given or lent to us by members of the public. The present publication is a reproduction of an official guide to Ballycastle, published around 1954 by authority of the Ballycastle Urban District Council. It has been scanned from an original copy and is of historic and nostalgic interest to the local community.

We are confident that this publication involves no breach of copyright, and we make no claim to ownership of future copyright. If, however, anyone feels they have a claim to the copyright of any of the material published here, please contact us through our website

As this is a reproduction of an earlier publication, we cannot take responsibility for errors that may have occurred in the original. We do, however, take responsibility for any that may have resulted from the scanning process.

All adverts are of historic interest only and have no present relevance in terms of product prices, claims or locations.

# Ballycastle

## for Happy Holidays.

# UPTON'S RELIABLE IRISH TOURS
## — LIMITED —

Offer you the Holiday of a lifetime with Headquarters at The Marine Hotel, Ballycastle, combining seven days' residence at this premier Hotel, nightly entertainments, (resident orchestra), the beauties of Ballycastle & District together with its opportunities for Golf, Tennis, Bowls, Fishing, Swimming, Boating and other sports, and over 450 miles of first class Coach Touring to the most interesting and romantic features of the Emerald Isle.

*SEVEN DAYS UNDER IDEAL CONDITIONS WITH NEVER A DULL MOMENT*

Ask any up-to-date Holiday Agency all about it or write to

*The Hotel with those extras so different from the rest*

# UPTONS RELIABLE IRISH TOURS Ltd.

TELEPHONE : BALLYCASTLE 210

# SIGHTSEEING TRIPS
# FROM BALLYCASTLE

•

*Ulster Transport provides a highly organised passenger service throughout Northern Ireland.*

*Visitors will find many facilities for short trips in the neighbourhood of Ballycastle and for more extended motor coach tours during the holiday season to various beauty spots and places of interest further afield.*

•

Further Information from:

## PASSENGER MANAGER

### Ulster Transport Authority

# 21 LINENHALL STREET :: BELFAST

# BALLYCASTLE OFFICIAL GUIDE

Published by Authority of Ballycastle Urban District Council

## CONTENTS

## ILLUSTRATIONS

Printed and Published by

J. S. SCARLETT & SON, Castle Street, BALLYCASTLE

**Copyright.**

1

Photograph by]

THE STRAND

[Judges, Ltd.

# Ballycastle

## for Happy Holidays.

In these days of recognised holidays for all classes of the community — industrial, commercial and professional — health and holiday resorts vie with each other in offering their particular attractions to the tourist. Some rely on natural surrounding's, where scenic gifts by land and sea have been particularly lavish; others have bought financial enterprise to bear on attempts to embellish these — not always with results satisfying' to everyone. For just as tastes differ in almost everything, so do they affect the choice of a holiday resort. Some people declare their preference for nature unadorned, while others look for those amenities and haunts of amusement which are features of the so-called up-to date seaside resort nr ill land hydro. It has been said that "it takes all classes to make a world," and to a certain extent something similar might be applied to the selection of a holiday resort — it takes all classes to justify the existence of so many, and the varied nature of their claims to preferment.

In a unique degree Ballycastle can lay claim to a combination of most of the amenities associated with health and pleasure resorts — in fact it has the attractions and facilities of urban, rural, and seaside surroundings, for its situation is in the midst of them all. Located on the fringe of a fertile and prosperous agricultural district, it enjoys a good supply or those products of the farm which certainly go to enhance the enjoyment of a holiday at the seaside — or anywhere else – and visitors are not slow to show their appreciation, particularly on the eve of their departure, for some have been known to take away many samples or the good things they enjoyed as holiday fare while in Ballycastle. The neat little town itself is only a couple or hundred yards from the sea, so there is some justification for the "Irishism" uttered by the man who declared — "You can be in the town and the country and at the seaside all at one time!"

---

3

**Incomparable Situation**. — Nestling snugly in the Valley of Glentow, one of the Nine Glens of Antrim, Ballycastle has an incomparable situation. Towering above the town is heather-clad Knocklayde (1,695 feet in height). Eastward, away to the right of the beautiful bay with its clear blue waters, the wondrous promontory of Fair Head stands up proud-looking and erect like a sentinel on guard. Out to sea is the fair isle of Rathlin, providing shelter from the full blast of the North Atlantic. Westward, jutting into the sea, is the shapely white head of Kenbane. The town proper is linked up with the Quay-formerly Margietown, a place of considerable importance in the days when the McDonnell clan held sway — by a magnificent broad avenue, the Quay Road. Here is provided a picturesque setting of woodland and architectural beauty, noble trees being flanked by well-planned and artistically-constructed villas, having frontal gardens ablaze with the choicest blooms. The varied colouring here is indeed striking and effective.

**A Model Resort.** — Municipal control is vested in an Urban Council consisting of twelve members elected every three years. Since its inception thirty-four years ago the town has made rapid strides as a seaside resort, numerous improvements adding appreciably to its amenities and the comfort of visitors. In every respect it can fairly claim to merit the distinction of being acclaimed a model resort. "Cleanliness is next to godliness" is an axiom strictly followed in Ballycastle. Its streets, footpaths and avenues are shining examples of it.

The town's health record should be sufficient to satisfy the most exacting tourist. It is singularly free from outbreaks of disease, and the death-rate is one of, if not the lowest in Northern Ireland. There are four reasons for this happy position — firstly, the town's healthy situation; secondly, its perfect sanitation — no town possesses a more efficient sewage system; thirdly, its excellent and abundant water supply, obtained through the Knocklayde reservoirs from springs in the neighbouring limestone; and lastly, its high-grade milk supply---probably due to the fine milk-producing qualities of the pasture land of the surrounding district.

Well-stocked and up-to-date business establishments are in the township, with their prices distinctly reasonable. Here, at any rate, there are no inflated prices during the tourist season. An up-lo-date Cinema seating five hundred, with every modern comfort and showing the best films continuously each evening, is available and conveniently situated.

Photograph by]

[J. Salmon. Ltd.]

BALLYCASTLE FROM THE STRAND

**Strand and Promenade** — The strand forms a mile of glorious sands stretching from where the river Margey enters the sea to Bath Lodge —situated in a picturesque residential quarter at the end of the Golf Links. A delightful promenade plentifully supplied with seating accommodation extends from the Harbour to the Bridge over the Margey at the Glass Island, which provides access to the beach and the Golf Links.

**Bathing Facilities**. — In this very necessary amenity the visitor is specially well catered for. The Strand is the ideal resort of those who enjoy the combined pleasures of surf and sun bathing, while the more adventurous may delight in the thrills of diving into the crystal clear waters of the Bay at the new Harbour. Then furtherer afield, particularly at the Pans Rocks, good bathing facilities are available. And the most satisfactory feature is the safety of the places at which bathing in indulged in-mishaps at Ballycastle are few and, far between.

**The Treasure Hunt** — Where people are seen walking along with bent heads and eyes the ground, the inference is that they are either in the doldrums or in deep meditation; and this spectacle is no uncommon along the Strand at Ballycastle. But these figures are not those of deep thinking mortals, immersed in reflections on the past, but searchers intent on present-day discoveries. in the form of stones which, with some knowledge in selection and skills in after treatment, may prove valuable. For, strewn along the; beach in considerable quantity, and constantly replenished by the vagaries of the tides, are numerous stones of varied size, colour, and description. Here is a veritable "happy hunting ground" for those whose tastes lie in that direction — and indeed for the novice and those who enjoy looking for things! For the information of the sceptical, it may be stated that valuable stones have actually been found and afterwards converted into handsome articles of adornment, their classification including crystal, cornelian, rose-quartz, blue agate, topaz-quartz, amethyst, quartz, etc. Polished and set, such can be made lasting and handsome) souvenirs of the holidaymaker's visit to Ballycastle.

Photograph by]

[J. S. Scarlett & Son.

THE STRAND AND FAIRHEAD

# PLACES THE TOURIST SHOULD VISIT.

**Glenshesk and Knocklayde** — The town's environment provides the pedestrian with a veritable wonderland of beauty and historic interest. What delights are in store for visitors to the captivating Valley of Glenshesk, four miles away. Here they can find a sequestered nook amid the fragrant hanging bells of the hyacinths and all the sweet virginal flowers of the glen, and there, in unalloyed happiness, surrounded by Nature's choicest gifts, live lightly for an hour or so in dreamland, Oblivious to the cares of life.

Then there is Knocklayde, on whose heather-clad slopes they can bask the live-long day and inhale the rarest of all air, the air of the mountain-top. What a glorious view, too, is to be obtained from the summit!

**Carrig - Usnach.** — In addition to its historic associations, Ballycastle has a connection with certain of the mythical hero tales of Ireland. The well-known "Three most sorrowful Tales of Erin" are "The Fate of the Children of Usnach," "The Fate of the Children of Lir," and "The Fate of the Children of Turenin," and in two of these the scene is part laid near Ballycastle. The first of these legends is a story of the first century, and describes the adventures of the beautiful Deirdre, who fled from the court of King Connor MacNessa at Armagh, with her two brothers and her lover, northward to Dunanynie and across the sea to Loch Etive in the Highlands of Scotland, where a spot is called "Dun MacUsneachan," the residence of the sons of Usnach. Tempted home by offers of pardon favour, the four returned and landed, after the absence of two years, on a projecting rock on the Shore east of Ballycastle which to this day is called Carrig-Usnach — the rock of Usnach. Here they were treacherously set upon and the three chieftains slain. This is popularly said to have been the first breach of faith ever perpetrated in Ireland; and the country people still point out the dark stains on the rock, which innumerable winter gales have never been able to efface.

"The Fate of the Children of Lir" tells of the adventures of Finola, Lir's daughter, and her three brothers — Aed, Con, and Fiachra; how they were transformed by a jealous step-mother into white swans and doomed to spend three hundred years each on the Sea of Moyle (the North Channel), Lough Davra (Westmeath), and Inis Gloria (Mayo) until the advent of Christianity by the sound of St. Patrick's Bell. It also relates the sufferings of the children in their altered shape and how they were frequently driven by gales from the Sea of Moyle into the sheltered pool at the mouth of the Margie. It is this portion of the legend that the poet Moore has immortalised in his "Song of Finola".

*Photograph by]*

THE MARGY RIVER

*[J. S. Scarlett & Son.*

"Silent, 0 Moyle, be the roar of thy waters,
Break not, ye breezes, your chain of repose,
While, murmuring mournfully, Lir's lonely daughter
Tells to the night-star her tale of woes."

**Fair Head.** — A visit to this majestic promontory — at the highest point 639 feet above the sea — should not be missed. It can be reached direct by road, but many visitors prefer the thrill — after traversing the winding roadway along the rocky sea edge with massive cliffs lining the inland side — of scrambling their way to the top. Of late the Golden Eagle has made Fair Head one of its haunts and bird watchers find their patience sometimes rewarded by magnificent views of this rare bird in flight over the stupendous promontory.

Proceeding along the summit, the famous **Grey Man's Path** is reached. This is a huge fissure which allows of a steep but practical descent to the base of the precipice. Over the chasm a great pillar — one solid stone — lies transversely. By descending to the foot of the path the visitor can obtain a proper idea of the amazing architecture of the promontory. From below, the stupendous columns of which it is composed tower up in cyclopean grandeur, presenting to the spectator the most magnificent colonnade ever erected by nature, and in comparison of which the proudest monuments of human architecture are but the efforts of pigmy imbecility to the omnipotence of God. Some of the great ribs of rock are 250 feet long and 20 to 30 feet in diameter; and the steep talus which slopes from the cliffs to the sea is composed of gigantic fragments, many of them as large as a cottage. Who the "Grey Man" was history does not relate, but he was doubtless the centre of some old-world legend of the time of the "three sorrows of Erin,"

From the summit on a clear summer's day a glorious panoramic view is unfolded, Ballycastle glistening in the sunshine, with Knocklayde towering behind; the while glitter of Kenbane; Carrick-a-Rede, and all the headlands stretching eastward of the Causeway. Further west the purple outline of the Donegal mountains rises clear on the distant horizon; northward Rathlin, its cliffs and heathery hills standing out gloriously against the blue sky; next the Scottish islands come in view the high bare hills of Islay; the famous Paps of Jura; and further eastward all the western shore of Cantire, rapidly nearing from a dim distance till it frowns, grim and bare, only fourteen miles away, and clearly come into view the lighthouse that guards this narrow passage and the few scattered cottages on the hillsides, Over Cantire, on the right, rise the misty hills of Arran; and off its southern extremity lies Sanda Island. Beyond this Ailsa Craig towers solitary and gigantic, with a dim backing of Ayrshire hills, which runaway southward as far as Carsewell Point, the last visible speck of Scottish land. By the direct roadway, Fair Head is about six miles from Ballycastle.

Photograph by]          FRENCH FISHING BOATS IN THE HARBOUR          [J. S. Scarlett & Son.

**Murlough Bay** — A little further from Fair Head is lovely Murlough Bay, enclosed by woods and steep wooded slopes. Here the visitor will find a scene of unspeakable grandeur. The beauty and diversity of the scenery is directly due to the remarkable assemblage of different geological formations in a limited area. No more ideal spot than this for pic-nic parties!

**Torr Head.** — A boss of rock, standing boldly out on the edge of tile sea, Torr Head, nine e from Ballycastle, is well worth a visit. The scenery surrounding it is enchanting, especially viewed from the tortuous road several hundred feet above sea level.

**Loughareema. Bay** — The subject of Moira O'Neill's famous poem, "The Fairy Lough," Loughareema, is an isolated moorland tarn better known as "The Vanishing Lake" owing to its proneness to become dry during the summer season. Several streams enter it, but none leave it, the water escaping by an underground passage or "swallow-hole" in the chalk rocks. After heavy rain the lake rapidly rises till it sometimes overflows the road, while in summer weather it runs entirely dry, and its muddy bottom presents an interesting geological study in the way of sun-cracks and miniature canons. It is situated almost on the summit of the mountain between Ballycastle and Cushendall, and about seven miles from the former.

## BUN-A-MARGY FRANCISCAN FRIARY

Of the numerous attractive features with which visitors to Ballycastle are impressed, the existence of many historical and interesting antiquities must be emphasised, for the resort and surrounding district can lay claim to more of these than most places: indeed, the locality is literally dotted with scenes of former glories and tragic happenings of the past. Among pleasure seeking visitors there are many of antiquarian tastes; and at no resort, perhaps, is there more scope for indulgence in this interesting pursuit than at Ballycastle and its environs.

One of the oldest historical landmarks--and one of those with which many outstanding events in early Irish history are associated-is Bun-na-Margy Friary, the well-preserved remains of which cover a goodly area quite close to the town, in what might now be called its suburbs. No wonder, then, that visitors with any historical knowledge at all — apart from antiquarian enthusiasm — enquire as to its location and take the few minutes' walk which brings them to the sombre but interesting pile of stone and lime which has withstood the ravages of centuries! As well might a visitor to Edinburgh come away without a tour of the Castle as a tourist here miss a visit to Bun-na-Margy!

Even an abbreviated history of the ancient Friary would be out-of-place and rather lengthy in a booklet such as this; but presumably it owes its origin to the MacQuillan Clan some time in the fourteenth century, before the MacDonnell ousted them from their holding in North Antrim. It is recorded that in 1639 seven hundred Highland Scots, refugees from the Covenanting persecutions of that time, were confirmed in the Friary by a Franciscan Father Bonaventine Magennis. At the west end of the church there is an old cross still standing which is supposed to mark the grave of Julia MacQuillan, the famous "Black Nun of Bun-na-Margy." Strange tales are still told of her deeds of piety and penance. The Friary has harboured in its time less gentle lodgers than the "Black Nun," for the warrior and his war-horse have been unwelcome visitors there. Often in the past have its peaceful aisles resounded with the din of battle.

The ground of its cemetery literally heaves with Clandonnen dust. Here were buried those who fen in the disastrous overthrow of Clandonnell at the hands of Shane O'Neill in 1565: and here, too, also rest those who died in the great battle of Slieve-an-Aura in Glenshesk, where the MacDonnells finally put an end to the resistance of the older lords, the MacQuillans.

In a little corner of the cemetery are the graves of nine sailors who lost their lives when H.M.S. Viknor sank in the bay on 12th January, 1915, torpedoed by a German submarine,. Here also are buried a number of soldiers and sailors who gave their lives in the 1939 - 45 War, so that side by side modern and ancient warriors lie sleeping. The altar stone of the Abbey, after being secluded in Glenshesk for many years, is now used in the Chapel of St. Brigid's Abbey, Ballycastle.

The preservation of the ruins has recently been undertaken by the Ministry of Home Affairs, Northern Ireland, in conjunction with the Belfast Naturalist Society (Archaeological Section).

**Carrick-a-Rede.** — Most visitors make a point of journeying to Carrick-a-Rede, five miles distant, to see, and if sufficiently intrepid, to cross the famous swinging bridge. During the salmon-fishing season, from March to Autumn, fishermen have to cross from the mainland to a small island opposite. To enable them to do this a bridge made of cables has been constructed from the edge of the cliff on the landward side to the island at a height of about 90 feet above sea level. Two cables are made fast at each end to iron rings rivetted in the rock, and these are lashed together by transverse ropes. Between these two main cables a floor of two planks width is laid from end to end of the bridge. Two ropes fixed to rings a little higher in the rock serve as hand-rails, but are really designed to give confidence more than support.

The bridge curves sharply with the weight on it, so that you go down a steep slope on entering the bridge and up a corresponding slope as you near the other end. To add to the thrill the crossing affords, if there is any wind the whole thing swings sideways in addition to springing in lively fashion under one's feet. It can, of course, be crossed with perfect safety by anyone who has a cool head, and the fishermen carry sheep over it when they want to take them on or off the inland.

## A ROUND TOWER.

Another of the pleasing features of North Antrim is the number of picturesque villages and hamlets with which the neighbourhood is studded, and many of them are within easy reach of Ballycastle. Particular interest should centre in Armoy, which, like Dervock, will have a special attraction for tourists, but with a different object in view. They will be interested to see one of the best preserved specimens of the ancient Irish round tower now remaining in the country. While time and decay have contributed to the disappearance of nearly all of these historic landmarks, the one at Armoy has escaped the effect of these ravages to a remarkable degree, and there it stands still proudly upright, to be seen by the onlooker, not as the poet Moore puts it, "in the waves beneath him shining," but tall and erect on dry land — and, to the people's credit be it said, a free sight, and not "syndicated," as some other historic objects are, for the sake of filth lucre! Again the visitor will be impressed with the beauty of the route to this interesting spot, for the six miles thither is through or past the hills and valleys of lovely Glenshesk, and for variety the return may be made by the shorter road around the other side of lofty Knocklayde.

## WHITEPARK BAY,

The Antrim coast is rightly famed for its picturesque bays and inlets, and no great distances separate one from the other. Ballycastle has its own stretch of curved land watered by the sea; and round the corner, so to speak, is the beautiful Bay of Murlough; but pride of place might doubtless be given to Whitepark Bay on the other side, between the Giant's Causeway and Ballycastle, and about six miles from the latter resort. A lovely strand, encircled and sheltered by verdant slopes and white cliffs, it excites the admiration of visiting motorists and bus passengers as they drive along the road which overlooks the beauty spot. "What place is that?" is a frequently-heard query, and anyone with local knowledge will take a natural pride in pointing out the beauties of the bay, with the neat little hamlet of Portbraddon nestling beneath the cliffs at one corner, while the clean golden sand makes a perfect curve to the other.

THE STRAND, LOOKING WEST

Photograph by]     [Judges, Ltd.

Well it is, perhaps, that such a beautiful and unspoilt world of nature is far removed from large centres of population, else its quiet charm and serenity
 might suffer the fate of other similar beauty spots and become the haunt of trippers with their unsightly litter, and be made the site of ugly shacks and caravans with the appearance of which we have become only too familiar at other places along the coast. Up to now the most familiar type of visitor are the geologist and the archaeologist, who — despite these ominous-looking titles — are harmless and welcome! In Whitepark Bay and its surroundings they have a wide field for their researches and enthusiasm; for many discoveries of historic and very ancient associations have been unearthed some, indeed, being said to reveal features of human and animal life in pre-historic time.

Whitepark Bay is now owned by the National Trust, who will preserve its beauties, and allow the public right or free access to it.

**Rathlin Island.—** There is no more delightful or interesting outing than that by motor boat to Rathlin Island, six miles from Ballycastle, provided, of course, sea and weather conditions are favourable. The island, seven miles long, having a right-angle turn in the middle, and about a mile in breadth, is old in history, Pliny and Ptolemy mention it as Ricnia. A monastery was founded there in Columbkille's day, but the exposed situation of the place made it a prey to Northmen, who sacked and burned it in 790. In 1576 and 1641 Rathlin was the scene of two terrible massacres.

It has earned a niche in history for having been the haven of Robert Bruce in 1306 after his defeat at Perth. His refuge on the north shore, now known as Bruce's Cave, is worthy of a visit, and none the less interesting is the fragmentary remains of Bruce's Castle, an ancient stone fort on the north-east shore. The latter, according to tradition, was the scene of the episode of Bruce and the six-times-baffled spider.

All the northern and western shores of the island are formed of grand basaltic cliff-ranges. Along the south-western shores the cliffs are formed in their lower parts of snow-white chalk in their upper portion of dark lavas, giving the durious appearance so conspicuously seen from Ballycastle, and to which Charles Kingsley refers in "Westward Ho" as noticed by Amyas Leigh and his Ship mates in their long chase after the Spanish Galleon: "A strange island, half black, half white, which the wild people called Raghery, but Cary christened it "the drowned magpie."

Photograph by]　　　　THE LAMMAS FAIR　　　　[J. S. Scarlett & Son.

The cliffs, especially those of the north-western end, are the sanctuary of multitudes of sea-birds, and during the breeding season a visit to Rathlin is amply repaid by a sight of these great bird colonies. Gulls, kittiwakes, herring-gulls, and great black-backed — come hither in flocks: razorbills and guillemots, both common and black, are present in thousands. The grassy slopes are honey-combed with the burrows of the puffins. The Manx shearwater nests in holes under the highest cliff on the island: and other non-gregarious birds, such as the raven, chough, peregrine and oyster-catcher, bring out their young in safety in the wild recesses of this rugged coast.

In 1898 Rathlin was used by the late Marchese Marconi as a wireless experimental centre. To-day it is linked up with the mainland by wireless telephone. There is one public house and no police station on the island; but despite this the inhabitants, whose occupations are fishing and farming, are peace-loving and not as they are depicted by the well-known Irish poetess, Moira O'Neill in her poem, "Rachray" —

"See Rachray Island beyont in the bay;
The dear knows what they be doin out there
But fishin' an' fightin' an' tearin' away;
An' who's to hindher an' what do they care?"

If these are the things they were "do in' out there" in Moira O'Neill's day — and that is very doubtful — times have changed on Rathlin; for a more industrious and kindly people it would be difficult to find anywhere. They bring their produce and their trade to Ballycastle, whose merchants recognise their proximity as a valuable adjunct to their business. The pity is that means of transport are not more favourable, but there are hopes and indications that this drawback may be remedied in the not too distant future. As it is, there exists fairly good motorboat connection, and both inhabitants and visitors make frequent journeys to and from the island.

In 1953 Rathlin Island was linked for the first time with the mainland by telephone.

**A Link with the U.S.A.**— Americans are often among the visitors to Ballycastle in the holiday season, and they may not all be aware that they are within easy distance of the ancestral home of one of their most illustrious Presidents — William McKinley. By the way, a rather pretentious guide-book for Northern Ireland gives a wrong and somewhat misleading location to this interesting spot, and it is not out of place here to indicate the exact locality. The old home is in the townland of Conagher, near Dervock, a pleasant and goodly-sized village within easy reach of Ballycastle. Indeed, the short distance thither is among the numerous enjoyable drives available to tourists in these parts; and when they reach Dervock — pleasantly situated on the banks of the River Bush — any of the residents will gladly direct

them to their "shrine", for they take a natural pride and will gladly direct
them to their "shrine," for they
take a natural pride in the fact that their district produced the ancestors of
one of the greatest statesmen that ever adorned the high office of President,
and whose memory is still revered by citizens of the great Republic.

## OTHER ANCIENT LANDMARKS

Two other old strongholds of the chieftains of other days may be
mentioned, both within easy distance of Ballycastle — the castles of
Dunseverick and Dunanynie. Little of either remains above ground, which
prompts the thought that if similar protective measures had been taken in
their case as have latterly been bestowed on other ancient monuments, more
of their architecture would be visible to the antiquarian and the tourist. As it
is, only a grim-looking stone wall on a prominent headland stands to mark
the site of Dunseverick Castle-and to indicate the skill of the builder and the
class of material used in those old days, for part of the structure remains
after centuries of the wild storms which beat in from the North Atlantic.

Dunanynie Castle has fared even worse. A projecting plot of ground
along the edge of the cliff, showing traces of ruins on its verdant surface, is
all that now remains of the once formidable castle. This stronghold on its
commanding site was used for purposes of defense from very early times.
Long before the castle of stone arose on the edge of the cliff, a deep ditch
and high earthen rampart repelled many a stubborn attack. In later times the
MacDonnells of Antrim made Dunanynie one of their favourite residences
and strongest retreats. It will be ever associated with the name of Sorley Boy
MacDonnell, Lord of the Route, who through storm and sunshine clung to
it and the little bay; and at last, having survived his enemies, he died
peacefully at the mature age of four score years and five, and was borne
from his sea-girt home to Bun-na-Margy Abbey. Access to this historic spot
can be obtained by the Clare Park grounds, a few minutes' walk from the
town, and one of the many enjoyable rambles in the neighbourhood.

So with these and other interesting relics of a storied and eventful
past scattered over the neighbourhood, we are tempted to drop into rhyme
of a sort, and write-

Ruins of castles and stately shrines,
To recall the glories of former times.
In this still favoured place abound.
And much of its soil is hallowed ground.

**Extended Excursions.** —Ballycastle provides a most convenient
base for more extended excursions, many places of notable interest to
tourists being within easy reach by both rail and road, including the

wonderful and far-famed Giant's Causeway, 10 miles by road; Portrush, 18 miles; Cushendun Caves, 12 miles; and Glenariffe Waterfalls, 18 miles.

**Past Glories**. — To-day Ballycastle is devoid of industrial activity. In the eighteenth century, however, it was a hive of industry. In 1736 Mr. Hugh Boyd, the land-owner, obtained from the Earl of Antrim a lease of all coal mines from Bun-na-margy to Fair Head. Within twenty years Ballycastle was an industrial centre. Mr. Boyd started upon the coal-bed which reaches from Murlough Bay to Glenshesk, where in 1770 his workmen broke into an ancient gallery which led to an extensive labyrinth of tunnels and passages made by seekers for coal at a very much earlier date, as may be inferred from the fact that hammers found in the workings were constructed of stone and the passages were encrusted with the infiltrations of a long period of time.

Mr. Boyd also built iron foundries, salt-pans, breweries, tanneries, and glass-works. The Irish Parliament lent assistance and spent over £20,000 in constructing a harbour. Ballycastle's future prospects looked bright; but on Mr. Boyd's death a dark cloud gathered which a few years later completely caused a blackout, for the industries one by one decayed and ultimately perished. What a tragedy for the town, and what might its future have been! Fitfully afterwards the collieries were opened up and prospered for a time, and then faded out. That the district is rich in mineral resources is unquestioned. New hope is engendered by the formation of a Committee for the purpose of developing industries in Northern Ireland, before which the claims of the district are being pushed forward; so that perhaps in the near future the town may regain some, at least, of its lost industrial glory.

Ballycastle had its great days, too, under Clandonnell, and many a stirring conflict raged in the locality, the fiercest being the two-day struggle ending in Slieve-an-Aura, five miles from the town, where the McDonnell's finally conquered the McQuillans.

## SOME POPULAR FESTIVALS.

Many well-organised sporting fixtures have been a feature of Ballycastle's provision for visitors during the holiday season; and while the restrictions and regulations consequent on two wars and their after-math have in recent years curtailed some of these, and caused the suspension of others, there are promising indications of revival, and the re-organisation of an energetic Amusements Committee has done much in this direction. The Annual Regatta and Sports was an old and very popular fixture which attracted crowds of spectators and representative entrants from a wide area. The venues for both the aquatic and athletic events were ideal for spectators and participants, and suspension of the fixture left a regretted blank in the season's activities.

THE LAMMAS FAIR

Photograph by] [A. D. McAuley.

21

The Lawn Tennis Tournaments on Ballycastle's famous grounds are recognised as amongst the best-organised in the North of Ireland, and these are again in "full swing." The Sports Committee have organised other amusement features which have proved most popular, including fireworks displays, band and other musical performances, fancy dress parades, and other such events enticing to visitors. These, judiciously distributed over the holiday season, cater for practically all classes of visitor, and are so arranged that some novel attractions are available at the periods when most people are on holidays,

For those who prefer actual participation in out-door sport Ballycastle has excellent facilities. No better golf course or bowling green of their size are to be found in Northern Ireland; and the good fellowship existing among the players — visiting and resident — is not the least pleasant and commendable feature of participation in these popular pastimes. Other sports are available to the holiday-maker. The athletes of Ballycastle are partial to football, hurling, and hockey, competitions in these games being frequently "run" in the summer. Spirited matches are "the order of the day," and sometimes well into the night; and many a clever exponent of these games has been "discovered" in the ranks of the local teams,

## THE LAMMAS FAIR.

By general consent the last Tuesday in August is regarded as the "biggest day" of the year in Ballycastle. For longer than the oldest inhabitant can remember that has been the date of the "Oul' Lammas Fair," as it is called in Ballycastle and in many places far outside the confines of County Antrim, and indeed of Northern Ireland; for the event and its associations are known not only to the people of the Six Counties, but to the innumerable visitors who have either "come for the day" or whose holiday sojourn has synchronised with the festival. Not a little of this fame and notoriety is doubtless attributable to the song with the familiar air and title which has become increasingly popular, and which was composed by a versatile and esteemed native of Ballycastle — the late Johnnie McAuley, whose genial personality is still lovingly recalled not only in his native town but throughout "The Glens."

To adequately describe the Lammas Fair would require much more space than is available in this Guide-Book; besides, it has so often been done before that even were the descriptions improved upon, it would still be a task involving repetition — and perhaps at the end "the half would not have been told." Suffice it to say that from early morn to dewy eve the crowds flock in by rail, bus, car, cycle, and on foot, until the town and its environs are congested; that despite this the best of good humour prevails; that stalls almost innumerable, laden with eatables and drinkables, augment the supplies in the "eating-houses" to good purpose; that public entertainers do the best they can and profit by it; that sellers of all sorts of gadgets give their wares glowing descriptions in picturesque language, and sometimes augment this form of persuasion by a demonstration; that police have a big enough job to control the traffic, and luckily — in recent years particularly — have little else to do; and that "on the morrow," before tired business-men are awake, the street cleansers have a busy time clearing up the litter so that Ballycastle may maintain its high reputation as a well-kept town. It has been suggested that sometimes these cleaners may have the chance to pick up odd coins dropped from careless or shakt hands around the stalls; but the infrequency of these windfalls would suggest that when people in this part of the country drop money they lift it again — or that if they don't, some keen-eyed friends have been helping them to look for it!

Lest it might be inferred from the foregoing that all is fun and frolic at the fair, it has to be recorded that the fixture well deserves its title through being one of the biggest sheep fairs in the North of Ireland, and dealers come from "all the airts" to compete at the auctions of the flocks which are driven in from a wide range of sheep breeding country. But few combine business with pleasure in these great gatherings; for sheep dealers and pleasure-seekers are well segregated, and while large sums of money exchange hands for prospective mutton at the Fair Hill, perhaps more — in smaller denominations, of course — are cheerfully spent on the good things obtainable at the stalls and in the shops around the town.

These stalls in themselves constitute perhaps the most prominent feature of the fair. How they compress the number into the spacious Diamond generally baffles the average onlooker, and the ingenuity of the official who marks out the "allotted span" for each would prompt the suggestion that his help would be invaluable in the new and fashionable task of town planning! Laden with fruit, sweets, biscuits, dulse — an edible seaweed dried and "cured" — and that mysterious but toothsome concoction styled "yellow man," these mounds of eatables, some of them built on the lines of the towering and neighbouring Knocklayde, would suggest an exaggerated anticipation of the peoples appetites; but by nightfall there is an astonishing clearance, and a speedy cheap sale at the finish sends the traders home with full pockets, empty boxes, and cheery faces! Not even the old call of the apple-seller was necessary — "A penny a pound, tuppence for a whole day's atin'." More money in the pockets or a better quality of merchandise may account for it, but it might be said — latterly, at any rate — that "no one is pressed to buy," and that trade is brisk the whole day long.

Photograph by]     THE STRAND, LOOKING EAST     [J. S. Scarlett & Son.

But we must not dwell further on the attractions — or distractions — of the Lammas Fair, however strong the temptation or wide the scope; so we will pass on to other phases of our main subject.

## FOR THE "SETTLERS."

The numerous amenities for the visitor mentioned in this booklet are available, with others added, for those who would desire to select the resort as a place for permanent residence. It has many advantages to offer — variety of scenery throughout a district studded with mountain and glen; facilities for sport and recreation; shops in which stocks are varied and prices reasonable; air which for purity and invigorating influences could in few places be equalled and in none surpassed; and a people courteous and cordial in their attitude even to strangers, yet homely and natural in their disposition.

As in all other places in these difficult times, vacant houses are at the moment practically non-existent — another indication of the popularity enjoyed by the resort — but this difficulty, like others, can generally be surmounted; and building ground is available on many desirable sites, and those in a position to erect their own dwelling should never have reason to regret their selection of Ballycastle as a place of abode. Water, sewerage, and electricity are laid on to these sites, or very near to them, which is a considerable advantage to prospective builders, and the rates, bearing in mind the conditions under which we at present live, may be termed reasonable.

The produce of garden, farm, and dairy is plentiful in Ballycastle, and much of it is brought to the town from the surrounding country and delivered "at the door" — a feature to be welcomed by the housewife as relieving her of anxiety as to its freshness! Another product which has lately been added by local enterprise is that valuable and scarce commodity — coal. In times gone by this was produced from the local mines in considerable quantity, some of it shipped to other parts, and much consumed by local industry and population. But a combination of ill-luck and untoward circumstances overtook the enterprise; the mines closed, and a few spasmodic attempts to restart output lacked the financial backing and mechanical equipment necessary to successful operation. Quite recently — and doubtless prompted by the scarcity and high price of the all important commodity — local "prospectors" have tried again with considerable success despite primitive equipment, with the result that at least some of the people have been helped to keep the home fires burning! There is a probability that coal may be produced in quantity that would at least meet part of the local demand; and that, in these times of scarcity, should be a source of satisfaction to the people of Ballycastle.

Photograph by] [J. S. Scarlett & Son.

THE GOLF COURSE

Fred Daly, British Open Champion and Ryder Cup Player, putting on the 13th Green, watched by Norman Drew, Walker Cup Player, John Glover, Irish International and James Henderson, Ulster Champion.

Photograph by]       THE TENNIS COURTS FROM THE PAVILION END     [J. S. Scarlett & Son.

# SPORTS AND PASTIMES.

In the realm of sport few towns are better equipped.

**Tennis**. Ideally situated facing the sea, on the site of the former harbour, are the ten grass and two hard courts of the Ballycastle Tennis Club, famed as the finest in the country. Two tournaments are held annually — one in the second week of July, and the other during August. The County Antrim Championships are decided — competitions which attract not only the leading players of Ulster but many from England, Scotland and Eire. Terms during June, July, August and September — monthly, £15s.; weekly, 10/ — ; daily. 2/6. Families — Monthly, £3; Weekly, £1 5s. Hon. Secretary — Mr. A. E. Green, Drumawillin House, Ballycastle.

**Golf.** Fronting the beach are the 18-hole golf links, and difficult it would be to find a more delightful or admirable setting for the game. The course is a thoroughly sporting one, and is most popular with visitors. It is, especially the greens, always kept in good order. Terms during June, July, August and September:— Gentlemen — 4/- per day, 20/- per week, 50/- per month; Ladies :— 3/- per day. 15/- per week, 37/6 per month. Putting only (all players) — daily, 1/6; weekly, 7/6. Sunday golf without caddies; charges included in weekly terms. Joint Hon. Secretaries — Mr. A. McCaughan, M.R.C.V.S., Strandview Road, Ballycastle and Mr. G. W. Scarlett, Glenshesk Villas, Ballycastle.

**Bowls.** Adjoining the Tennis Courts, there is the beautifully situated Bowling Green of the Ballycastle Club. The turf is excellent and is kept in first class condition. Visitors are welcomed as temporary members on the following terms:— 9d. per hour; 2/6 per day; 10/- per week; 15/- per fortnight, and 25/- per month. Rink Competitions open to Visitors are held during May, June, July and August.

Football, Hockey and Cricket Clubs are always delighted to arrange matches with visitors.

## FOR THE ANGLERS.

It may safely be assumed that among the numerous visitors to Ballycastle are members of the angling fraternity — that patient and expectant class of individual often referred to as disciples of Izak Walton! Here again the resort can claim to cater for all classes and conditions of men — and women, too, for angling is another of the sporting pursuits which a number of "the fair sex" have taken to — with more or less success! Those who desire to catch fish — or fail in the attempt — can have the wish gratified by sea and land, so to speak. There is plenty of sea, and lots of vantage points from which to ply the craft; while those who take the short journey to Fair Head — another of the attractions which no visitor should miss — can have the spice of variety added to an enjoyable outing by "whipping" the surface of the lakes there to entice and deceive the trout with which they arc said to be well stocked. Permits to fish these lakes are necessary, and can be readily obtained on reasonable terms. Sea fishing can, of course, be indulged in to the heart's content, "free, gratis and for nothing," and a similar advantage attaches to efforts made to coax trout from several "burns" which meander through the district round about. The Glen and Carey rivers are constantly being restocked with trout and permission to fish these rivers call be obtained on application to:— Mr. A. F. McCoy, I. D,S., Quay Rd., HON. Secretary Ballycastle & District. Angling Club. Boarders who don't want to give the fish away can rely on the landladies to "cook the' catch." or see the task performed by an understudy!

# EDUCATONAL FACILITIES.

Higher Education is provided by two seminaries —

**The Ballycastle Grammar School** (Telephone 254) — a day school (mixed) — occupies one of the most up-to-date and best equipped (educational buildings in Northern Ireland. The curriculum, which covers all the usual subjects, includes also practical courses in experimental science, domestic science, art, and manual instruction. The School has its own playing field and pavilion, and also has the enviable record of having won the Ulster Schoolboys' Hockey Cup eight times within thirteen seasons.

**The Cross and Passion College** — a modern boarding and day school for girls — occupies a healthy and picturesque situation and has extensive grounds attached for games and athletics. The course of studies embraces the usual subjects taught in the best Irish and British secondary schools.

**Technical Education** is provided in the form of a Day Junior Technical School. There are also afternoon and evening Technical Classes in Commercial Subjects. Evening Technical classes are provided in Shorthand, Arithmetic, English, Woodwork and Domestic Science. There is also a class in Tractor and Motor Car maintenance,

# PLACES OF WORSHIP,

**St. Patrick and St. Brigid's Catholic Church.** A fine building in Gothic style, standing on an open elevated site at Avenue Road. The work of erection was undertaken by the late Most Rev. Dr. McAlister, when parish priest, and in 1870 the church was consecrated by the late Most Rev. Dr. Dorrian. The tower, spire and bell were erected during the pastorate of the late Very Rev. John Conway, P.P., V.F., and extensive improvements, including the laying in mosaic of the sanctuary, were made by the late parish priest, the Very Rev. Bernard Canon Murphy, P.P., V.F.

**Ballycastle Church (Church of Ireland).** This church, which is situated in the centre of the town, was erected in 1756 at the sole expense of Colonel Hugh Boyd of Ballycastle. It cost practically £4,000, and is built on a site adjoining a castle erected by Sir Randall MacDonnell, first Earl of Antrim, about 1620. This castle fell into ruin soon after the rebellion of 1641, and not a single trace of it now exists. The church formerly was roofed with small local slates or tiles and is built in the Graeco-Italian style. Five bells, cast by Lester & Pack, London, were installed in 1760. On top of the Octagonal spire there is a weather-vane, and on the Lower a clock with one dial facing west. On the south side of the tower there is a sundial, the various hours of the day being cut on the freestone wall of the tower.

**Ramoan Parish Church (Church of Ireland).** This church was built in 1849. The style of the building is early English. The Church is situated on the outskirts of the town. Rector — Rev. J. N. Goulden, M.A.

**Culfeightrin Parish Church (Church of Ireland).** This church built in the later English style and consecrated in 1831, is situated about 1½ miles from Ballycastle on the Cushendall road. Rector Rev. J. R Brady, M.A.

**Presbyterian Church.** The site of the Presbyterian Church is at the apex of Castle Street. The first minister was Rev. Samuel Lyle, ordained in 1829, and the present is Rev. J. C, Culbert, B.A., L.L.B.

**Methodist Church.** The first Church was built by Mr. Hill, Hillhead, Ballycastle in 1793. The present Church, situated at the junction of Market Street and Avenue Road, was erected in 1830 and the manse adjoining in 1863.

**Gospel Hall.** This building is situated on the Coleraine Road, and was erected in 1917.

**War Memorial.** An obelisk set in a cul-de-sac off the Quay Road perpetuates the memory of the many residents of the town who lost their lives in the First Great War.

# GENERAL INFORMATION.

**Population:** Winter, 3,000.        Summer, 6,000.

**Early Closing:** Wednesday.        **Market Day:** Tuesday.

**Cattle Grading:** (Ministry of Agriculture) Thursday.

**Banks:** Belfast Banking Co., Ltd. ; Ulster Bank Ltd. ; Northern Bank, Ltd.

**Post Offices:** Quay Road, open from 9 a.m. to 6 p.m. (open on Sundays from 9 to 10-30 a.m.) and Sub-Office at Bayview Rd. Deliveries — 8.30 a.m. and 2 p.m. Dispatches 8-15 a.m., 3-05 p.m. and 5 p.m. (latest English Mail). The Town is well supplied with pillar boxes and telephone kiosks.

**Correct Postal Address:** Ballycastle, Co. Antrim.

**Telephone Exchange:** Open day and night.

**Police Barrack,:** Market, Street.

**Bus Service Depot:** Railway Road. Telephone: 365.

**Rathlin Motor Boat Service:** Boat leaves Pier at 10 a.m. on Mondays, Wednesday and Fridays (weather permitting). Return Fare, 5/-. Trips for privat3 parties arranged.

**Cinema:** Market Street. Continuous nightly.

**Urban Council Offices:** Castle Street. Telephone: 225,

**Electricity Office:** Castle street., Telephone: 260.

**Public Library:** Castle Street.

**Food Office:** Castle Street. Telephone: 274.

**Church Services:** Presbyterian Church — Hours of services: Sabbath 11-30 am.. and 7 p.m. Ramoan Parish Church (Church of Ireland), Ramoan Road — Hours of services: Sunday, 11-30 a.m. and 6-30 p.m. Ballycastle Church (Church of Ireland), The Diamond — Hours of services: Sunday, 8-30 and 11-30 a.m., Evening Prayer 6-30 p.m. Culfeightrin Church — Hours of Services: 11-30 a.m. also at 6-30 p.m. during summer months. S.S. Patrick and Brigid's Catholic Church, Avenue Road _— Mass : Week-days, every morning at 8 a.m.; Sundays, 8-30 and 11 a.m.; also at 10 a.m. during summer months. Evening Service at 7, except on second Sunday of each month at 6 p.m. Methodist Church — Hours of Services: 11-30 a.m. and R p.m. Gospel Hall Sprvic8 eV81Y Sunday at 11-:10 a.m.

**Lammas Fair:** Last Tuesday in August each year.

**Annual Holiday:** Wednesday after Lammas Fair.

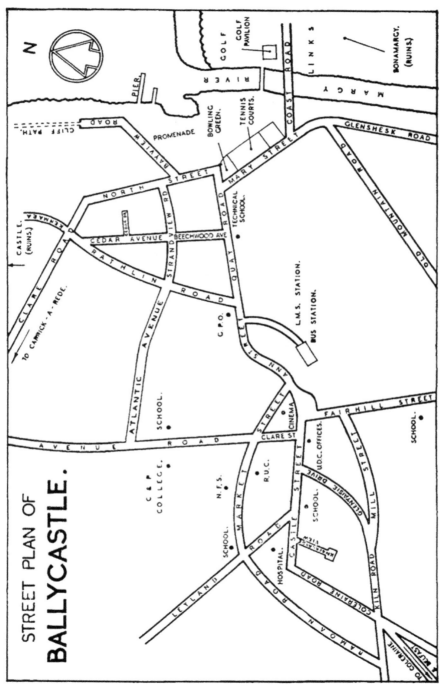

STREET PLAN OF
BALLYCASTLE.

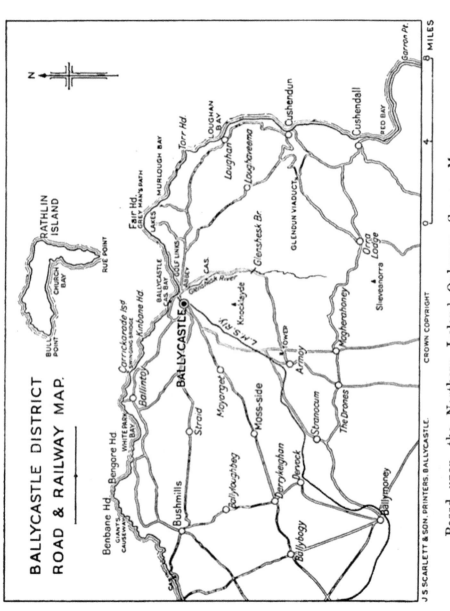

# BALLYCASTLE DISTRICT ROAD & RAILWAY MAP.

N

RATHLIN ISLAND

BULL POINT

CHURCH BAY

RUE POINT

Benbane Hd
Bengore Hd
GIANTS CAUSEWAY
WHITE PARK BAY
Carrickarade Isd
SWINGING BRIDGE
Kinbane Hd
Ballintoy

Fair Hd
GREY MAN'S PATH
MURLOUGH BAY
Torr Hd
LOUGHAN BAY

LAKES
GOLF LINKS
BALLYCASTLE CAS BAY
ABBEY
BALLYCASTLE CAS.

Bushmills

Ballyoughbeg

Straid

Mayoget

Moss-side

Derrykeghan

Derreck

Ballybogy

Ballymoney

The Drones

Stranocum

Armoy
TOWER
Knocklayde
L.M.S RLY.
Glenshesk River

Loughan
Loughareema
Glenshesk Br.

Cushendun
RED BAY
Cushendall

GLENDUN VIADUCT
Magherahoney
Orra Lodge
Slieveanorra

Garron Pt.

0        4        8 MILES

J S SCARLETT & SON. PRINTERS. BALLYCASTLE.        CROWN COPYRIGHT

Based upon the Northern Ireland Ordnance Survey Map with the sanction of the Controller of H.M. Stationery Office.

# BALLYCASTLE GOLF COURSE.

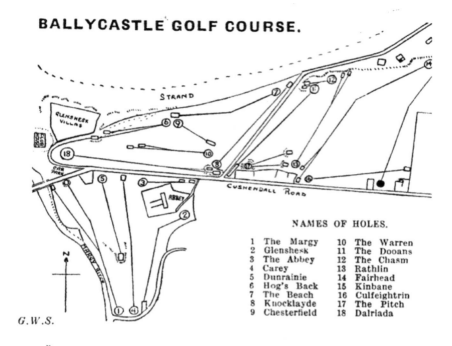

## NAMES OF HOLES.

| | | | |
|---|---|---|---|
| 1 | The Margy | 10 | The Warren |
| 2 | Glenshesk | 11 | The Dooans |
| 3 | The Abbey | 12 | The Chasm |
| 4 | Carey | 13 | Rathlin |
| 5 | Dunrainie | 14 | Fairhead |
| 6 | Hog's Back | 15 | Kinbane |
| 7 | The Beach | 16 | Culfeightrin |
| 8 | Knocklayde | 17 | The Pitch |
| 9 | Chesterfield | 18 | Dalriada |

*G.W.S.*

# BALLYCASTLE GOLF CLUB

The Eighteen hole Course is one of the most interesting in Ulster. Nature has provided an ideal setting where the plus Golfer and the long handicap man can equally enjoy themselves.

Open Competitions are held every week from June to September; VISITORS ARE ESPECIALLY WELCOME The length of the Course is 5742 yards. Bogey 71.

Further details can be had from the Hon. Secretaries: Mr. A. M'CAUGHAN, M.R.C.V.S., Strandview Road or Mr. G. W. SCARLETT, Glenshesk Villas, Ballycastle

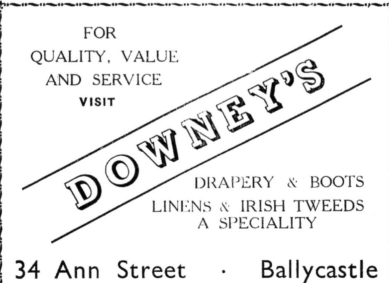

*On top —*

## for quality

Many a year has passed since Inglis started to make biscuits. It takes time, experience and skill to make a perfect product. Inglis believe that they have gone a long way to achieving this. Inglis have got used to shortage of ingredients; but out of what Inglis can use comes a galaxy of delightful shapes and sizes, each blended with goodness and baked to perfection.

Many a year will pass before you can find better.

## INGLIS

*Quality Biscuits*

Inglis & Co. Ltd., Belfast

## Other Clachan titles of interest in North Antrim

- *Songs of the Glens of Antrim* - Moiré O'Neill
  Written 'by a Glens woman in the dialect of the Glens, and chiefly for the pleasure of other Glens-people'.
- *Travels In Ireland, Part 4*, Dundalk, Newry, Belfast, The Antrim Coast, Rathlin, The Giant's Causeway – J.G. Kohl
  Impression of the North East Coast of Ulster, as seen by a German visitor the year before the Great Famine.
- *Handbook of The Seventh World Ploughing Contest of 1959*, Armoy, Northern Ireland,

## Also of interest

- *Travels In Ireland* - J.G. Kohl
  A very readable account by a German visitor of his tour around Ireland immediately before the Great Famine.
- *Distressed Ireland – 1881* - Bernard Becker
  A series of letters written as the author travelled around the West of Ireland, visiting key places in the 'Land War'. We meet Captain Boycott and other members of the gentry, as well as a range of small farmers and peasants.
- *A Journey throughout Ireland, During the Spring, Summer and Autumn of 1834,* - By Henry D. Inglis
  Inglis travels Ireland attempting to answer the question, 'is Ireland and improving country?' using discussion with landlords, manufacturers and tenants plus his own insightful observations.

clachanpublishing.com

Clachan Publishing, Ballycastle, County Antrim.
Email; info@clachanpublishing.com,
Website: http://clachanpublishing-com.

Lightning Source UK Ltd.
Milton Keynes UK
UKHW021540100521
383469UK00013B/2601